Slipping Through the Cracks

Parent, Professor, and Pastor's Guide for College Students

Thomas Ask

For the glory of God.

Printed in the United States of America

Contents

Keep your heart with vigilance, for from it flows the springs of life.

Proverbs 4:23

Preface

Launching children into the real world is scary. College takes a role in that transition for many families. The college experience presents both good and bad things. Because you are reading this, you probably think the good things outweigh the bad things. This is not a discussion of how to make college cheaper, more efficient or change the culture, rather it is an introduction on how we can make the intimidating, worrying transition from home to college smoother for the child who loves Christ. If you are a professor, you are asking, "How can I improve the student experience from a Christian worldview?" If you are a pastor, I really commend you for concerning yourselves with the flock that are "over the horizon" and traditionally left to their own devices. Thanks for caring about this vulnerable phase of a young person's life.

I'm writing this because I'm old. I'm sixty years old and have been a faculty member for twenty-one years. I'm also a dad. I have a grown, college-educated son and daughter. I have a wonderful wife, who shares great wisdom, love, and insights. Currently, I'm a professor of industrial design, which is a peculiar mix of art and engineering.

I have been an advisor for two Christian organizations during most of my faculty years. I have worked with a lot of new students, worried parents, cringing professors, and outreaching pastors. My Christian worldview has been awkward most of the times and an occasional battle has arisen. These are tough days to be a biblical literalist.

I am not a pastor or theologian. Readers come from many backgrounds and I can't presume to provide the theological insights presented by your pastors.

This book is divided into four parts. Feel free to skip the parts you don't like. I tried to lay out a case for the applications provided at the end of this writing. The flow of logic makes sense to me, but it may be pedantic and burdensome, so deal with the material as you like.

Some writing notes: I generally stick with the term *college* over *university* or *higher education* for readability. Also, I use *professor* rather generally, but the intent is to standardize on this commonly recognized term for all those who teach at college level, regardless of academic rank.

I have divided parents, professors, and pastors into separate chapters, but I hope you will peek into those chapters that aren't about you—I think you will find them helpful. The writing is more stuffy and pretentious in some places, more conversational in others. I hope you enjoy the variety.

Thanks for joining me as we strive to love young people and not let them slip through the cracks as they go to college.

Part I

Welcome to College

A man sees in the world what he carries in his heart.

Johann Wolfgang von Goethe

Slipping Through the Cracks

1

Introduction

You lay in bed thinking about your child. *What is he doing? Where is he right now? Is she lonely? Is she overly-stressed?* The worry is deep. Your mind swirls with a mixture of memories, negativity, hope, and imagined threats. The cauldron of worries is stirred by one of Macbeth's witches and you smell the nervous sweat. But there you are, lying in bed doing nothing. Your actions are—nothingness. You just worry. You're used to taking action. A part of you wants to be there for them, buried in the moment—a comforter. You want to be the one that can still hold their hand like when they were little. You want to walk next to them, speaking of playgrounds and toys. But now you have only worry as a companion. You miss the smiles and giggles and being able to walk side by side.

Parents deal with this anxiety quietly. The hole in their heart is real but it's covered by the world's distractions, where every moment is assaulted by technology and noise.

Many decades ago, I was taking an engineering design class. The professor had us sit in alphabetical order. I got to the class early because my previous class was next door. I couldn't see the far side the long blackboard because my name started with an "A" and I had to sit at the end of the front row. I asked the professor if I could move so I could see the blackboard. He said, "No." He was a good professor, but he had his rules.

A few years ago (long after he passed away), I was nostalgic and looked him up on the internet. I found out that he been an active member of an evangelical church. I had no idea he was a Christian. Christian professors can have cranky rules, but still it would have been nice to know. For me, that was an age of stress, loneliness, and confusion masked as confidence. I was looking for role models and there weren't many. Perhaps he thought, as I do now, that he would be vulnerable to exploitation if he acknowledged his Christian faith. He would have to be nice, not ruthless. He would have to be a Christian on display. I don't like that vulnerability now, and I'm sure he didn't want that burden. Instead, a mentor is lost among the math calculations and declarative statement of a mechanical engineering class.

Students enter college looking for a new community as they try to fit in. They are striving to cast away vestiges of childlike behaviors and act maturely as defined by youth culture. They have a radar out for what the culture is like around them. They look to harmonize their self-identity with what they are immersed in. They lose their face-to-face connections with old friends and organizations, not to mention their family. On the academic side, they may face new ways of learning and difficult coursework. They may quicky become disillusioned with their academic program as they take classes that don't seem related to their major.

It's easier to watch a noisy video than read this book. But let's take time together and look at this period of transition. Let's look at what happens in college life. Let's look at the role of parents, professors, and pastors in the transition from home to college. It's not easy. There are a lot of smoke and mirrors that make it seem easier than it is. Your child is nervous, but that emotion may be hidden under a thick mask of contrived joy. However, the anxiety doesn't mean there isn't hope. Students should be optimistic and full of hope for the promises of a college education.

2

A Great Start

You wouldn't be reading this book unless someone dear to you had already decided to go to college or you are closely connected to a college. I wanted to offer encouragement before considering the challenges for parents, professors, and pastors,

College education is useful. Data shows this. More importantly, it offers *hope*. It opens enchanting doors. Taking hope from someone is the cruelest fate. I have spent over four years overseas, mainly in developing countries, where many young people don't have hope for getting out of their current situation. I have seen many of these situations, but I will share just one.

Nearly forty years ago, I was in central India, trying to find the backpack that a criminal group had thrown off my train. I was checking the area around the railroad track where the train slowed down to negotiate a curve. It was in the middle of nowhere. There were several simple lean-to shacks in the area where people lived between the railroad tracks and the farm fields. I walked past one lean-to home and a man lifted up his baby. He had a big grin. He was very proud of the baby. The man's wife came out and sat next to him. No Westerners came to this remote place. I was an oddity. The man wasn't trying to get money from me or engage in any kind of hustle. He was just a proud dad. He had a wife and a baby, and a roof over his head. I thought about that baby, what opportunities would he have to move away from gathering coal along the railroad track?

That baby had a proud father and didn't care about where he lived. But I wondered what he would dream of when got older. What would the baby hope for when he grew up? Happiness and hope can be separate things, but a part of us dies when we can't aspire for something.

Late night conversations and brain-burning calculations can be part of the college experience. Being swamped with work and packed with stress can draw out some great abilities. I wouldn't want to go back to those times, but they do offer a lot of intellectual challenges to someone trying to use their abilities to make a difference in the world.

Education and training are different things, some want to learn a specific skill and trade, some want a broad-based general education. You don't want a physics professor to fix your furnace, and you don't want your mechanic to create a quantum computing system. Certain roles are uniquely suited to us. Moms are the best moms, dads are the best dads—you don't want the sociology professor next door doing any of those things.

Some Data

Let's look at the data that supports going to college.

According to the US Bureau of Labor Statistics, those with bachelor's degrees earn almost $30,000 more per year than those with only a high school degree. A Georgetown University study showed that college graduates earn 1.2 million dollars more over their lives than high school graduates. Specifically, the study says those with less than a high school degree earn 1.2 million over their lives, those with a high school degree earn 1.6 million, and those with a bachelor's degree earn 2.8 million. These are median values and the range is very broad, especially for those with college degrees.

Income varies widely based on major, with STEM and healthcare occupations earning the most.[1]

College graduates also have better job security. According to the US Bureau of Labor Statistics, college graduates have an unemployment rate half of those with a high school degree (2.1 versus 4.6 percent in 2021).[2]

According to a Pew Research study, college graduates are more satisfied with their work and less concerned about their jobs being outsourced. According to this study, about forty percent of high school graduates are concerned about outsourced jobs versus thirty-two percent for college graduates. This study found that "job satisfaction varies by household income, education, and key job characteristics. And the way people feel about their job spills over into their views of other aspects of their lives and their overall happiness."[3]

A college education opens many doors and draws out the mind's richest potential. Students join a community of ambitious people who share similar goals. The blended group of high school students breaks into communities focused on science, art, healthcare, engineering, education, and the humanities. We are encouraged when we are surrounded by like-minded people. They push the performance bar higher and organically create a culture that nurtures the mind.

Students are delightfully surprised to be in the company of so many others think like they do and share the same goals.

College has allowed many people to move into the professional ranks and enjoy satisfying and useful work. However, we often follow contorted paths. Life is not as linear as it seems in our youth. The Danish theologian, Soren Kierkegaard wrote, "Do not fly so high with your decisions that you forget that a decision is but a beginning."

However, education provides a distinctive mental preparedness for whatever awaits. When referring to the passion to immediately participate in life "with all the strength of his soul," the Russian novelist Fyoder Dostoevsky wrote:

> Young men do not understand that the sacrifice of life is, perhaps, the easiest of all sacrifices in many cases, while to sacrifice, for example, five or six years of their ebulliently youthful life to hard, difficult studies, to learning, in order to increase tenfold their strength to serve the very truth and the very deed that they loved and set out to accomplish—such sacrifice is often almost beyond the strength of many of them.[4]

3

College Life

In addition to education, college is a halfway house for parents to hand off their children. It promises a bed, meals, structure, community—and an education that has value. These promises are ancient, going back to the universities of Nalanda, Paris, Oxford, and Al-Azhar, where children of the elites were sent to learn. The students would gain knowledge of language and literature then move to exploratory thinking. This education was coupled with learning social graces and developing elite networks.

Some "Great Books" programs still exist where students learn from the writings of deep thinkers and creative geniuses who have weathered the test of time. More commonly, vocationally-oriented universities meet the needs of working-class students and hungry industries. This education has been a valuable steppingstone for many of us, moving us into the professional class where we could pursue challenging careers. The applied sciences were my refuge for a safe, good-paying career as an engineer.

Many professors have a true heart for students, a passion for education, and a desire to help individuals overcome obstacles. There are some, especially without metrics of success outside of academia, that view their professional success as simply getting students to agree with them. They want proteges to adopt their worldview and thereby extend their minds into those of the youth put under their care. I have heard this type of talk, where faculty say with pride how they modified a student's understanding of something. In some ways this can be good, but a richer goal is for students to hear a range of ideas and extract their own insights—not have them imputed by someone who has an unfair advantage to the podium (and grading!). I had a professor who would assign article readings with opposite thoughts about a topic. He handled complex problems fairly. It was so well done, I could never discern his personal opinion.

Problems with College Culture

The Apostle Paul found a college-type gathering in Athens at Areopagus (Mars Hill) in Acts 17. There he encountered people that enjoyed discussing new ideas, saying, "We wish to know" (Acts 17:20). When he preached the gospel, there were three responses: some believed, some were intrigued, and some mocked him (for teaching about the resurrection of the dead). This seems like a reasonable outcome. Regardless of the outcome, they let Paul speak. Contrast this to Acts 21 where Paul speaks at the Temple in Jerusalem. There they "seized Paul and dragged him out of the temple, and at once the gates were shut" (Acts 21:30). This response happened elsewhere, for example earlier in Acts 17 when he was preaching in Thessalonica. He presented a view that was different than their religion. Rather than free expression and debate, he was not allowed to speak. Which one represents the modern college?

We will consider some of the external pressures of colleges that affect how they operate, but let's do an initial overview of the situation among faculty and administrators.

Faculty

Generalizing about faculty is somewhat unfair, but I wanted to offer a few insights. The work is unique because of the autonomy. Faculty can have loving and gracious hearts for students and energetic focus and commitment to their discipline. This is not always the case, some are condescending to students and seem to relish their clear status difference. Some faculty focus on research, some on teaching. Most faculty do both.

The college culture is one that preserves privileges long gone in private industry, such as special parking privileges and academic ranks. Professors want better parking than students and rationalize any special status with some altruistic wrapping. The procession of ranks moves from tenure-striving, hard-working, *assistant professor* to nationally impactful *professor*. Many faculty want their titles worn publicly, Dr. "so and so" or Professor "so and so." With these honorifics, hierarchy is preserved and the status conferred by twenty-somethings feeds into the know-it-all nature of many faculty.

However, it is not so dire. Through the mire of control, most professors want to teach students and wish to challenge them and let their minds wrestle with difficult ideas. "The hottest fires make the strongest steel" applies to one's mind too. So if a nice professor holds a student's hand through every calculus problem, the student never struggles, never learns, and merely checks an academic box without his or her mind being challenged. Faculty differ on their approach to teaching. In college education, cases can be made for a variety of techniques because the students are experienced and sophisticated in their pursuit of knowledge and experience.

Efficient Education

Should colleges be super-efficient? What does that really mean? When an AI prompts us with a recommended word or a succinct answer to a query, we forfeit something—but it isn't our time. We seem to gain time with this added "efficiency". Efficiency is not what I am considering in this discussion and is beyond the scope of this writing. However, it is an important backdrop.

Tuition cost is not a proxy for quality. High tuition is often thought to indicate high quality. Colleges give "scholarships" to offset this so the student perceives a bargain. The education business model doesn't get real market pushback, colleges can fix finances by asking the government and students for more money. They can dig into endowments or impose upon parent and grandparent's savings.

The power distance is great between students and their college. They have no control on how it is administered. Consequently, students borrow more money and pay what they are asked. Of course some schools, especially small, private colleges without endowments, do feel economic pressures profoundly. Many have taken dramatic steps to increase enrollment, including eliminating admission standards. Whatever demographic and market shifts arise, prestige universities are safe, competitive state universities are safe, but lower tier institutions will be affected by financial pressures.

Non-educators' involvement in education has changed the educational culture away from its focus on the mind. Moreover, their added overhead expense has increased tuition. This change is rapid. One example is at Yale University, where the number of managerial and professional staff that Yale employs has risen three times faster than the undergraduate student body during the last two decades.[1] The rapid rise of the administrator-to-faculty ratio points to the changing heart of the university.

Administrators are usually talented and motivated. They take pride in their job. Because their job is not teaching, it is something else. That "something else" becomes a big part of the college experience for both students and professors.

Administrators don't enjoy the same protections as faculty. Many don't have backgrounds that translate well into private industry and they can feel trapped in the cultural bubble of academia. However, many colleges have huge endowments so they are financially isolated from the concerns of the business world.

Other external factors affect educational culture and efficiency. In another chapter, we will consider the federal structure of "conditions" that rose as a clear tool in the Supreme Court decision South Dakota v. Dole.

Slipping Through the Cracks

Part II

What Happened?

The heart has its reasons, which reason does not know.

Blaise Pascal

Slipping Through the Cracks

4

Church

Reverend Heinemann was my childhood pastor. He told us exactly what God said, or so it seemed. He spoke only biblical truths and didn't put up with anything else. He was a fierce protector and presenter of God's Word. When I grew older, my church presented the Bible with softer edges. The loving guidance of the Sermon the Mount took over the stuff that wasn't so sweet. Things that were culturally offensive were silenced. Expository, verse by verse, preaching withered. Culture moved one way and many churches tried to go along. They tried to be relevant, they tried to fit in. But what were they fitting into?

Americans' membership in houses of worship continues to decline and is now below fifty percent. In

2020, forty-seven percent of Americans said they belonged to a church, synagogue, or mosque, down from fifty percent in 2018 and seventy percent in 1999.[1]

Of course, the church will not fall, it is protected by Christ. In Matthew 16:18, Jesus promises the endurance of the church and that "the gates of hell shall not prevail against it." However, there is a disciplining, but when God's people look to him for truth, they will endure. In 2 Chronicles 20, God's people feared the attacks of their enemies, but said, "For we are powerless against this great horde that is coming against us. We do not know what to do, but our eyes are on you."

Christians don't wish to engage in a culture war, we want to change hearts. This starts with biblical truths. These truths are under attack within the church. This has been an ongoing change and we all encounter our own tripping point, where we can go no further.

Early in my college teaching career, I was the advisor for a Christian group that was aligned with nearly all the community churches. Sounded good. However, with time, I realized that many denominations had drifted from biblical truths. As I reflected on my role, I realized I could not serve this organization anymore. Sometimes interdenominational work is a rush to limit Christianity to the fewest beliefs. So few that everyone can agree. Is that the goal? Everyone agrees? The Nicene Creed was developed to push back false teachings, not to reduce the Bible to a few sentences. Now I am the advisor for Cru, which holds to Scriptural inerrancy.

At some time, our faith is challenged. We ask ourselves, *what do I really believe?* Do I believe what my church is saying, do I believe in what my denomination is saying, do I believe in what my culture is saying? I came to a point of saying "no" to all of these. This came after carefully thinking through the changes underfoot and comparing it to the Bible. It was really a beautiful experience when, at the age of forty-nine, I realized I didn't agree with what my church denomination was doing. That work of the Holy Spirit, as I sat in my recliner reading Galatians, is a sweet memory.

I didn't know where we could go for Christian worship, but I knew my family had to go elsewhere.

5

Parents

This chapter is short. Parents haven't failed their children like the institutional drifts of colleges and many churches.

Parenting is tough. But the family reflects God's plan for society (see Genesis 1:28, 2:24; Deuteronomy 6:6-7, 20-25.) The family also illustrates the relationship between Christ and his people (see Ephesians 5:22-33; Luke 15:11-32).

Your work and abilities don't magically create your children's outcome. Some peaceful parents have troublesome children, some troublesome parents have sweet children. It's not a math equation. But parents are a stronger institution than colleges. Parents love most unconditionally and strive to be wise. But they rely on institutions at various points. Do they trust this doctor, this teacher, this pastor? They make judgements as they juggle their personal needs and aspirations with the demands of their children.

Then comes the day. Your child is grown up and ready for the next step. Their ambition might amaze you as you may feel you have become weary from years of work and grinding routine. Now you need to trust in an institution to a degree you haven't before—an institution that says they will educate your child, as well as feed and house him or her. They will gather possible friends around him or her and place them in front of a professor.

I made a painting a few years ago that included the cycle I had observed in my own kids. I had the movement from being a baby to adulthood described by two paths. My painting has a purple sky and green valley. A branch extends across the long canvas and ends in a single leaf. I have the following words, indicating stages, painted over the landscape. They represent a feeling and a response to that feeling. This up and down cycle attempts to summarize our encountering evil and responding with a type of goodness.

Child →
Wonder →Discouragement →Interest →Disappointment → Complacency →
Adult

Child →
Happiness →Meanness →Kindness →Evil →Manners →
Adult

Babies are full of wonder and happiness, but they end up being complacent adults with good manners. A little sad, but true. However, Christians believe there will be another day when every tear will be wiped away.

Biblical parenting is presented by much wiser people than me. However, parenting is rooted in biblical truths, such as the commandment for children to honor parents, as well as the guidance that parents are not to exasperate their children. When Jacob was struggling to make a place in Israel, his sons listened to his instructions even when they were fully grown. So did Noah's children and most of the other Bible heroes. It seems that deference can't be expected now, sort of like David and his son Absalom, who rebelled and modeled his father's weaknesses instead of strengths (see 2 Samuel 15).

Parental actions are rooted in a mixture of scriptural obedience, love, and wisdom. No rule book lays out a clear path. The most beautiful part of God's promises is that he loves your children more than you.

Yes, we get to pray to the one who gave his life for them. As a child goes off to college, parents are left largely with a spiritual role. We pray. We must pray.

6

Colleges

College cultures are much like Thomas Jefferson's inner struggle—his learning and rationality didn't bring him a salvation of his mind. Jefferson spoke of ideals, he wrote about ideals, and then lived a very different life. His rationality and lack of a real foundation let him slide along the muddy path of the degenerate man.

Charles Malik, former President of the United Nations General Assembly and one of the authors of the UN's *Universal Declaration of Human Rights*, opined, "The university is the clear-cut fulcrum with which to move the world. More potently than by any other means, change the university and you will change the world."[1]

Colleges are important, they influence society. Almost all political and business leaders start their journey by going to college. Many people have developed their political and moral philosophy in college. During their college years, students compare what they learned as children against the broader canvas of ideas.

A Brief History

Colleges have long had a connection with religion. While there is disagreement about which university is the oldest, it may well be the fifth century Indian Nalanda University. Nalanda was connected to Buddhist teaching and was the center of learning in much of the ancient world.

The United States' premier universities, such as Harvard, Yale, and Princeton started as institutions for the training of clergy. Harvard was started by the Puritans of Massachusetts, Yale by Connecticut Congregationalists, Princeton by New Jersey Presbyterians, Brown by Rhode Island Baptists, and Dartmouth by New Hampshire evangelicals. Harvard's earliest motto was *Veritas Christo et Ecclesiae* (Truth for Christ and the Church). Harvard changed dramatically following the death of important leaders at the turn of the nineteenth century. It became dominated by Unitarians in 1805. This is a benchmark date for the secularization of the American universities.

The western tradition of higher education started with the medieval universities, such as Bologna, Paris, and Oxford. These universities were closely connected with the Christian church. In 1231, Pope Gregory IX issued a bull connected to the University of Paris. He asserted the role of the university as being part of the "weapons of the Christian soldier" in developing learned clergy.

> Paris, the mother of sciences, ... a city of letters, stands forth illustrious, great indeed, but concerning herself she causes greater things to be desired, full of favor for the teachers and students.... There the iron is raised from the earth, because, when the earthy fragility is solidified by strength, the breastplate of faith, sword of the spirit, and the other weapons of the Christian solider, powerful against the brazen powers, are formed from it.[2]

The Italian poet Francesco Petrarch (1304-1374) is considered the founder of the Renaissance. Motivated by what he considered the "Dark Age" corruption of the church that dominated society, he looked for enlightened insights from Cicero and other ancient writers. Petrarch was fascinated by their unveiled perspectives and embraced the idea of learning from the ancients. He initiated the rise of renaissance humanism, which led to a return to direct study of ancient texts, including literature, history, and moral philosophy. Humanists sought well rounded learning that could be applied to the secular world.

Even with the rise of science as the means of learning about the world around us, the notion of the university being the home of inherited knowledge lasted until the nineteenth century. Universities evolved closer to their current state as they transitioned to scientific pursuits and a more forward-looking perspective. They also abandoned any connection with religion or transcendent truths. The long serving president of the University of Chicago (1929-1945), Robert Maynard Hutchins, wrote:

> When men begin to doubt whether there is such a thing as truth or whether it can ever be discovered, the search for truth must lose that precision which it had in the minds of those who founded the American universities. And if the traditional notion of freedom, when dragged up out of our subconscious, looks less impressive than we had always supposed it would, free inquiry ceases to be that infallible guide to terrestrial salvation which our academic ancestors thought it was. We must now confess that the beacons established to

illuminate the pathway of our people give a light that is flickering and dim. The universities, instead of leading us through the chaos of the modern world, mirror its confusion.[3]

The move from humanism to science coincided with the development of public research journals that encouraged scholars to share their findings as well as greater access to universities by the general public.

Petrarch was a singular voice that critiqued a deeply rooted system. Critiques can be helpful, but the press of professed experts can have a deleterious effect. While most work can be improved by the critique of others, there are categories of work in which we don't want the communal input. We don't want the university. We want to be a solitary songbird in the forest. Poets and other creative practitioners may work best in their quiet ecology of introspection and creative expression.

False Promises

A well dressed, well-spoken admissions officer told us with a straight face that they read all the student admission essays at an Ivy League college we were checking out—all 35,000 essays.

How many people do you need to read and evaluate 35,000 essays every year? They had an eight percent acceptance rate. Why would they bother to read essays from students that didn't meet other criteria?

This was a ridiculous and deceptive proclamation. The sad part is many applicants spend hours and hours perfecting their essay. Clearly the essay wouldn't matter for many of them, but the high school students were deceived to think so.

I don't know what they do with these essays. Logically, they use them for borderline cases and other program goals. Maybe they use keyword searches, discourse analysis, or AI driven evaluations. Surely they don't read most of them, but they told the students and their families they *read* them all. The sad part of this deception is the false promise it makes and the wastage of applicants' time.

Colleges have long promised more than they can deliver. These promises have prompted court cases. For-profit colleges have been the most notorious. Recently, the Federal Trade Commission started pursing the most problematic colleges. Federal Trade Commission Chair, Lina Khan said, "For too long, unscrupulous for-profit schools have preyed on students with impunity, facing no penalties when they defraud their students and drive them into debt."[4]

However, non-profit colleges have similar problems, perhaps toned down a bit, but the same. Just because someone attended college doesn't mean they will live happily ever after. This isn't the fault of the educational system, it is just the reality of marketing driven, mass education. Buyer beware.

Constraints on the College

Colleges are like companies—they are not people. Colleges don't have intrinsic morals. They are not people and therefore do not have the ability to make judgments like people. They are controlled by their own governance and external regulations, which are connected to the culture and society around them.

Constraints and standards move in unpredictable ways. Legal rulings in the United States have increased federal control of many parts of our society. Consider this summary of a United States Supreme Court's decision that affects how the federal government extends itself. In this case (South Dakota v. Dole) the Supreme Court ruled the government could require the state to raise its minimum drinking age as prescribed by the federal government or else have their transportation funding withdrawn. This is an interesting case to present and consider some of the actual wording as it offers us a detailed lens into the federal control of so much of our lives. Some of the specific findings written by the Supreme Court for this case read as follows:

> *Held:* Even if Congress, in view of the Twenty-first Amendment, might lack the power to impose directly a national minimum drinking

age (a question not decided here), § 158's indirect encouragement of state action to obtain uniformity in the States' drinking ages is a valid use of the spending power.

(a) Incident to the spending power, Congress may attach conditions on the receipt of federal funds. However, exercise of the power is subject to certain restrictions, including that it must be in pursuit of "the general welfare."[5]

This ruling allows a direct imposition of federal regulations by means of conditions. It pushed federal regulations to the local level. This power of "funding conditions" applies to private companies also. For example, federal contractors require vaccinations of all subcontractors so the contractors can retain federal funding.

These funding conditions have been used to impose federal requirements. We are paid to give up our rights. That is, the conditions of earning money become connected to other things that the government has decided upon. These funding conditions evade constitutional restrictions.

Lawful avenues for restrictions and regulations come from the legislature or the courts. Binding statutes come from legislature, while binding judgement come from the judiciary. Conditions don't have constitutional grounding. Conditions don't bind people and therefore evade scrutiny. In this way, the administration of money becomes a tool for control that lies outside the control and guidance of many modes that allow public scrutiny. This includes violations of conditions, which are often adjudicated informally. Private organizations regulate as a proxy for the government—you want our money, you follow our rules.

The privatization of regulations is a dangerous trend. Regulations don't bind legally, they exchange money. They are a gift with a request attached. This approach opposes the anti-commandeering doctrine put forward by the Supreme Court.

Another big external influence on colleges are accreditation agencies. These agencies provide external quality control systems that strive to ensure a level of rigor and acceptable curriculum. Commonly, a college will earn a regional accreditation and a major or program will earn a programmatic accreditation. Accreditations are important because they allow students to receive Federal financial aid, transfer credits, and gain professional licensure. Accreditation requirements govern much of undergraduate coursework. If a student has a question as to why they are taking a certain class, the answer is often because the class is required for accreditation.

There is increasing concern with accreditation agencies' ability to focus on student outcomes rather than measurable inputs (e.g., number of books, faculty credentials, governance.) While accreditation agencies limit the flexibility a program or college has in changing their curriculum or course structure, they do provide a type of independent oversight.

Colleges are affected by more than just federal incursions and the oversight of accreditation bodies. The social changes in our culture and a college's intellectual ecology also produce a distinctive environment. Our society is decreasingly connected with churches and there is also increased political tribalism and entrenched classes of victims who view the world through a narrow lens of their own making.

The Power of Stories

College culture is also influenced by the power of stories and history of judgements. Social psychologist Edgar Schein found that culture can be preserved by shared stories that "reaffirm the organization's picture of itself, its own theory of how to get things done and how to handle interrelationships."[6]

Stories of faculty or students being punished for saying or writing something are widely available. The Foundation for Individual Rights and Expression (FIRE) is one source for many stories. They also list the "Worst Colleges for Free Speech."[7]

The Americans Civil Liberty Union (ACLU) also provides useful guidance on free speech on campus and considers court cases that offer guidance on permissible expression. Their guidance is logical and follows the long tradition of free speech on campus. For example, their response to bigoted speech is as follows:

> Bigoted speech is symptomatic of a huge problem in our country. Our schools, colleges, and universities must prepare students to combat this problem. That means being an advocate: speaking out and convincing others. Confronting, hearing, and countering offensive speech is an important skill, and it should be considered a core requirement at any school worth its salt.
>
> When schools shut down speakers who espouse bigoted views, they deprive their students of the opportunity to confront those views themselves. Such incidents do not shut down a single bad idea, nor do they protect students from the harsh realities of an often unjust world. Silencing a bigot accomplishes nothing except turning them into a martyr for the principle of free expression. The better approach, and the one more consistent with our constitutional tradition, is to respond to ideas we hate with the ideals we cherish.[8]

Aren't colleges only concerned with the mind?

Two hundred years ago, the German poet, novelist and scientist Johann Wolfgang von Goethe opined that, "every day we should hear at least one little song, read one good poem, see one exquisite picture, and, if possible, speak a few sensible words." Now students are more likely to hear some simplistic slogan, read an STD warning, see an offensive advertisement, and write a social media update.

Colleges interrupt the development of the mind with many topics that might be characterized as indoctrinating rather than educating. We speak of critical thinking and synthesizing ideas but then immerse students in topics related to becoming "a better person." These tend to take the form of health issues and contemporary social challenges. While well-meaning, these programs do not nurture critical thinking skills and repeat similar information from secondary school.

If we conduct a seminar on the importance of physical fitness, we are taking time that the student owns and, to add to the indignity, asking them (or taxpayers) to pay for it. Are we presuming the student never had health and physical education in earlier years? Compulsory, non-academic training in all its forms makes the same presumption: You are ignorant, we have the truth; you will pay and give your time to learn our truth. Shouldn't an adult student be able to make these decisions?

Colleges have increasingly developed paternalistic attitudes toward students, compelling them to learn about lifestyle issues, whether directly, through subsidized speakers and signage, or through the reach of their academic programs. Students might question colleges' concern with physical fitness when, at the same time, residence halls offer all-you-can-eat buffets. These eating arrangements don't promote healthy eating and are financially unfair to women, who typically eat less than men. At the same time, colleges have embraced the entertainment business as a source of revenue and vehicle for recruitment.

Studies in the humanities and social sciences can nurture a student's mind. When carefully crafted to avoid indoctrination, they compel students to think deeply. They provide helpful interpretive approaches to gaining knowledge and offer alternate methods of inquiry outside of the scientific discipline's positivistic framework.

Colleges best serve the student and the public when they tend to the mind of the student and discard unilateral proclamations and allow students to speak "a few sensible words," to quote Goethe again. However, we must appreciate that colleges have done great things. They are vehicles for important research that has improved knowledge and solved problems. They are institutions that have nurtured students' minds and compelled them to think critically and gain discernment and wisdom. Colleges provide communities of like-minded thinkers that learn from each other and are encouraged by these social networks.

Dorm Life

A more immediate problem than what arises in the classroom is what arises in the dorms (or residence halls, if you prefer). I put this presentation last, because it is one of the oddest social structures around—put a bunch of young people together and see what happens. Colleges inherited this problem because it is immensely practical and attractive to have a packaged living and dining arrangement at the college. The transition from home to college can't be much simpler in terms of logistics. In addition, many dedicated residence advisors and residence life professionals work to ensure an appealing living environment. However, there are problems. These range from comfort and health[9,10] to roommates.

But the biggest challenge is peer pressure and the establishment of social norms. Personal experience has given us all insight into this behavior. Social norms, or normative influence, are powerful. The American Psychological Association's definition of normative influences resonates strongly with most parents' experiences:

[Normative Influences are] the personal and interpersonal processes that cause individuals to feel, think, and act in ways that are consistent with social norms, standards, and conventions. Normative influence is partly personal, because individuals who have internalized their group's norms will strive to act in ways that are consistent with those norms. It is also interpersonal, because groups place direct and indirect pressure on members to comply with their norms. Those who consistently violate the group's norms are often subjected to negative interpersonal consequences (e.g., ostracism, ridicule, punishment), whereas those who conform are typically rewarded.[11]

Being dropped into an environment that tends towards the lowest common denominator never seems like a good idea. There are lots of horror stories, I'll share one lesser one from when I went to college, over forty years ago.

I was in a triple room when I was an incoming college freshman. One of my roommates used marijuana recreationally, whereas me and my other roommate did not. The drug using roommate was motivated to get us to use marijuana to assuage his conscience. I declined this easy entree into marijuana usage. My roommate did not. He took to marijuana with alacrity. He flunked out of college in the first year.

Some people can handle drugs and continue their studies. For example, the roommate who got my other roommate started on drugs. I suppose seeing the stoned roommate passed out in our dorm's bathroom was informative. But the exposure to this depravity, and so much more of the ugly part of life, at barely eighteen years of age is sad and it is rooted in an institutionalized system of education that has allowed dorm life to be what it is. This isn't just a story to instill worry, it is one of many facts about dorm life that has gone on for generations. But there is always hope and informed action.

In addition to normative influences experienced in the intimacy of dorm life, other groups develop in college that form into subcultures. Studies have found group members need to protect the positive image of their group to satisfy the self-esteem they derived from the group. Groups will act in ways that protect their group regardless of facts.[12,13] These are powerful sociological forces working on students. Students need subcultures that embrace truth and the best elements of human character, such as sacrificial love.

Slipping Through the Cracks

Part III

Preparing For the Road Ahead

Memories are the key not to the past, but to the future.

Corrie Ten Boom

Slipping Through the Cracks

7

Biblical Preparation

How do you prepare children for college? Scripture prepares our hearts and minds for what is required. In 1 Thessalonians 5:14-18, the Apostle Paul packs a lot of guidance in a short reading. The reading below tells us to pray without ceasing (for you parents!) and encourage the fainthearted (for you professors!)

And we urge you, brothers, admonish the idle, encourage the fainthearted, help the weak, be patient with them all. See that no one repays anyone evil for evil, but always seek to do good to one another and to everyone. Rejoice always, pray without ceasing, give thanks in all circumstances; for this is the will of God in Christ Jesus for you.

Christians want Christ himself, not just the gifts he provides. We treasure Christ above all things and he is the object of our faith. We trust him to give us what we need the most, not just good stuff. Therefore, the consequences of our faith are not revealed in whether things turn out good or bad for us, but rather how they let us model Christ. Sanctification is looking at Christ without the veil that Moses was required to wear in hiding God's glory. We look at God's glory in Jesus and are encouraged as we try to love him. Loving can mean suffering. Romans 8:18 says, "For I consider that the sufferings of this present time are not worth comparing with the glory that is to be revealed to us."

Jesus connects our suffering with his suffering on the cross directly:

> The Son of Man must suffer many things and be rejected by the elders and chief priests and scribes, and be killed, and on the third day be raised." And he said to all, "If anyone would come after me, let him deny himself and take up his cross daily and follow me." (Luke 9:22-23)

Therefore, the scriptural admonition is to pick up the cross daily (gulp!) and accept the death of reputation, comfort, security, and health for something greater. The Apostle Paul spoke of his losses in Philippians 3:8, writing, "For his sake I have suffered the loss of all things and count them as rubbish, in order that I may gain Christ..."

Our fallen nature tries to ensure our comfort, reputation, and worth. However, 2 Corinthians 4:16-18 says:

Though our outer self is wasting away, our inner self is being renewed day by day. For this light momentary affliction is preparing for us an eternal weight of glory beyond all comparison, as we look not to the things that are seen but to the things that are unseen. For the things that are seen are transient, but the things that are unseen are eternal.

The sacrificial element of Christian life is a testimony in its own right. The Roman Emperor Julian was bothered by how the Christians of the fourth century were behaving. He noted these early Christians had no beggars and they "care not only for their own poor but for ours as well."[1]

A.W. Tozer wrote very directly about overcoming our fearfulness. Commenting about a man who lamented that religion should not interfere with his private life, Tozer wrote:

> To which we may reply that things have come to a worse pass when an intelligent man living in a Protestant country could make such a remark. Had this man never read the New Testament? Had he never heard of Stephen? or Paul? or Peter? Had he never thought about the millions who followed Christ cheerfully to violent death, sudden or lingering, because they did allow their religion to interfere with their private lives? But we must leave this man to his conscience and his Judge and look into our own hearts. Maybe he but expressed openly what some of us feel secretly. Just how radically has our religion interfered with the neat pattern of our own lives? Perhaps we had better answer that question first. The man with the cross no longer controls his destiny; he lost control when he picked up his cross. That cross immediately became to him an all-absorbing interest, an overwhelming inter-ference.[2]

Christian professors can be alone in the desert. This was immediately what happened to Jesus after he was baptized—he was in the wilderness where he would be tempted by Satan for forty days (Matthew 4:1-11). As soon as he starts his ministry, he is in a barren place with only Satan chewing at his heels. Jesus was weakened from fasting, and separated from a supportive community. Sound familiar?

The Apostle Paul was also in a desolate place. He was a well-educated Jew working among Gentiles. He sacrificed his familiar community, his reputation, security, and so much more in order to present the gospel. There is much that we can learn from how Paul handled that situation, but let's consider a couple of Old Testament stories that illuminate how God's people operated in a foreign land.

Brave Queen

Esther had a rough life. She was orphaned and raised by her uncle Mordecai who loved her dearly. They were living under the reign of Persian King Ahasuerus and they were trying to make their way in this world where they had no authority. Esther ends up as queen and has some influence in the king's life. As it turned out, Mordecai had saved the king's life at one point and was remembered for this. Both of these situations, being queen and saving the life of the king, worked together so when a law was put forward saying that all Jews would be killed (King Ahasuerus didn't know Esther was a Jew), Esther was able to intervene. But it was at risk to her own life. "If I perish, I perish" she says in Esther 4:16. She had it good, but realized that there are times God puts you in a position to act (see Esther 4:14). Esther not only acted bravely, but she also recognized she was in a unique position to do so.

Fiery Furnace

Another insightful story about the cost of Christian life is shown in Daniel, when the three Jews, Shadrach, Meshach, and Abednego, would not bow to a golden idol set up by King Nebuchadnezzar of Babylon as described in Daniel 3. They were threatened to be thrown into a furnace and burned to death. Their response:

> O Nebuchadnezzar, we have no need to answer you in this matter. If this be so, our God whom we serve is able to deliver us from the burning fiery furnace, and he will deliver us out of your hand, O king. But if not, be it known to you, O king, that we will not serve your gods or worship the golden image that you have set up. (Daniel 3:16-18)

The God whom we serve is able to deliver us. In this case, the three Jews lives were rescued, but this story points to our spiritual rescue by Christ.

Tough stories. But these two stories had happy endings. Not all biblical stories have physical rescues. Most of the apostles are executed. Jesus is killed, even after he prays mournfully that he be spared. In the garden of Gethsemane, Jesus says, "Yet not what I will, but what you will" (Mark 14:36).

And so, Jesus is executed. But the painful death does not hold him—he rises again.

Providence and Luck

Many biblical stories reveal how a cascade of bad events turn to a salvation story. These events show God's control on our lives and how his providential works operate. We often view the immediate reaction to our work rather patiently noting the long term affects.

An ancient story is instructive here.

An old farmer had worked his crops for many years. One day his horse ran away. Upon hearing the news, his neighbors came to visit. "Such bad luck," they said sympathetically. "Maybe," the farmer replied.

The next morning the horse returned, bringing with it three other wild horses. "How wonderful," the neighbors exclaimed. "Maybe," replied the old man.

The following day, his son tried to ride one of the untamed horses, was thrown, and broke his leg. The neighbors again came to offer their sympathy on his misfortune. "Maybe," answered the farmer.

The day after, military officials came to the village to draft young men into the army. Seeing that the son's leg was broken, they passed him by. The neighbors congratulated the farmer on how well things had turned out. "Maybe," said the farmer.

8

How Do We Know?

We all need to gain insights into the range of approaches used in establishing foundational knowledge that governs how we act. Those of us who wrestle with faith, reason, and culture may be attracted by the commonly held assertions within the social sciences that knowledge arrives at us through our own interpretation. That is, we process the world around us through our personal lens. Human knowledge is not absolute; it has to be related to the position of the receiver and is influenced by culture and biases.

Francis Bacon opined about human values and preconceptions intruding into science. He was especially contemptuous of religion's connection with science. In his essay, "The Four Idols," he holds religion in contempt. However, his argument is that "the formation of ideas and axioms by true induction is no doubt the proper remedy for keeping off and clearing idols."[1] What is induction? In Bacon's view, it was gathering and categorizing facts that lead to a truth. Who gets to decide what a fact is? How do you obtain facts about the transcendent, which by definition is beyond the sentient and can't be measured?

Philosophy considers the general nature of reality (metaphysics) and the study of knowledge (epistemology). Metaphysics is a broader term for ontology, which seeks to understand the fundamental truth about existence. For Christians, these inquiries are faith-based. God is the answer to the metaphysical question, "What is the true or ultimate nature of reality?" Specifically, the Father, Son, and Holy Spirit are in essence (ontologically) equal; however, they exist in a functional (economic) state with distinctive roles and relationships. God's revelation is the answer to the question, "How do I gain knowledge about the metaphysical?" This revelation is the Bible (special revelation) and nature (general revelation). The Bible also answers the ethical question of moral philosophy — what is right and wrong.

There are three basic types of thoughts regarding how we gain knowledge. This domain of study is called epistemology and can either assert:

1) Knowledge is obtained by observation and measurement. *Materialism* is a common term for this.

2) There is no absolute truth and all knowledge is created by humans. Humans create their own truth. This is sometimes referred to as *anti-realism*.

3) Divine revelation. This is a religious appeal based on revealed beliefs about God. [2]

The philosophies of science establish a foundation for the study of nature. But a battle exists about the undergirding philosophy of science. Does science operate in an environment where scientists quickly abandon previous theory in the face of evidence, or is science founded on traditional mental models and group behavior? Two schools of philosophy champion each side. Karl Popper and others argue that science always includes new evidence while Thomas Kuhn and others assert that social forces impede changes to scientific theories.

Some philosophers have extended this inquiry into the limits of scientific method. They argue that the outcomes of revolutionary times in science, such as the acceptance of the Copernican sun-centered (helio-centric) model for the solar system, occur when traditional theories are being strongly challenged. During these times, scientists will resist abandoning their traditional theories. Moreover, when science moves beyond its realm of studying the world of nature, it is not doing science but rather abiding the philosophical view of scientism. Scientism asserts we are rationally entitled to only believe what science claims, science is the only (or best) route to truth and meaning.

Data usually drives theories, from grounded theory approaches in the social sciences to inferential statistics. However, data, or in a general sense, evidence, are a product of data acquisition methods. Evidence is also routed through biases connected with how we obtain data and the context under which we acquired it. All these issues are a threat to objectivity. The interface of evidence and bias can be summarized by the German physicist Werner Heisenberg's assertion that "the world cannot be separated from our perception of it."[3]

Science is not the only discipline in which foundational principles have to be considered. Philosophy itself has the "principia" of human reason. Therefore, philosophy has to be founded on theology. Why? Because theology has its foundation based on God and God's revelation. That is the starting point for understanding ultimate truths, and it is founded in faith. A nasty loop when your only god is reason.

We recognize that scientific advances are not always orderly. Some philosophers[4,5] would consider the whimsy and chaos of individuals as productive and powerful agents of change. Others[6] considered some final truth to be unattainable or even desirable, which points back to the eighteenth century Scottish philosopher, David Hume's realization of there being no end point in proving scientific theories. He argued that the contentious and muddy world of scientific pursuit is good.

Scientists strive to extrapolate theories beyond what is reproducible. These make intriguing conjectures. Interpretive research frameworks, as used in the social sciences, simply recognize that facts and theories are founded on faith in employing human reason and interpretation. We can use qualitative methods to do research, but it requires an articulated framework describing an understanding of how the world works and how you can learn about how it works. Research should (but rarely does) require a positionality statement. This statement is helpful because your position with respect to data influences acquisition methods and interpretation, among other things.

Our personal attitudes affect data acquisition and processing. Researchers recognize a long list of potential biases as they battle this challenge. Many of the names are self-explanatory, such as: selection bias, social-desirability bias, and confirmation bias, to name a few examples.

As a Christian, I don't follow ontological naturalism (the view that the supernatural does not exist) as a guide. Ontological naturalism can't handle the notion of possible human irrationality. It has a faith component, namely, that the human mind is rational and can be a tool for acquiring and processing information.

Approaching knowledge from an interpretive perspective lets us make ticklish forays into science and recognize its limitations. We can join the company of philosophers who recognize that science has faith in human reason. The Bible says our minds are naturally hostile to God (Romans 8:7) and non-Christians will view theological approaches as foolish (1 Corinthians 2:6-16). Faith in God and the illumination of the Bible comes from the Holy Spirit, and Christians can boldly assert this as the first page of their mind's journey. We articulate our "framework" and move on.

Part IV

What Can We Do?

Be strong and courageous. Do not be frightened, and do not be dismayed, for the LORD your God is with you wherever you go.

Joshua 1:9

Slipping Through the Cracks

9

What Can Be Done?

Our cultural norms remove parents' legal controls and even powers of persuasion when their children are emancipated from the household. The education industry gets into the emancipation business by easing the transition, which is very attractive to both the nervous parents and the aspiring college students. However, education has many meanings. A common response to societal problems is "more education." Soon we have seemingly been educated about a wide variety of ills that extend outside our community and country and into all the remote regions of the world. We have had our awareness risen by media-rich adventure events. But do these things strike the soul? Do they even create new ideas or ways of thinking? It seems like much of this awareness-raising is just more of the advertising world into which we are submerged, where we are being shouted at by people who tell us what to buy, what to wear, what to eat, what to say, and ultimately what to think.

We live in a highly curated world of information, whether it is obvious, such as the librarian's decision about what books to buy and display, or the invisible and insidious, such as Google's listing of "best responses." Curation might be rooted in a parent's deep love or a professor's deep concern for the mind. Some curation is intended to present personal views or wide-ranging "out of the box" ideas. Wide ranging ideas sound good, but the most outlandish are cut without comment. For example, when my students evaluate possible solutions to a complex case study, say a boss who is doing something wrong, one solution should be, "kill the boss." But students never come up with that solution. It is self-censored. Students feel some things shouldn't be said, they have a sense of propriety and a moral compass. But this internalized guidance comes from various sources.

Who can help in this transition to college and what can they do? Let's take a look at some of the people and institutions closely connected to young adults—they can make a difference.

10

For Parents

The student peeked through the door of my class studio. It was late Friday night, when I would take my kids to the studio for our "Friday night, party night" when we would play games, make things, and watch videos.

The student extended his leg through the door and cautiously entered—his parents tucked behind him. It was the Friday before our Fall semester started. They were taking one last tour of the campus before the parents would drive off. I could sense the anxiety. The parents and student talked with me and didn't want the conversation to end. And then it did. I could feel the ache.

Parents will always remember the final separation from their kids, whether it be a last hug at the dorm room, or waving to them as they drive off. I remember the ache of leaving my own children. I remember needing a long, mournful walk in the woods behind our house each time I returned home from first dropping our kids off.

But I easily remember a more distant time, over four decades ago, when my sister left me alone in the dorm with my two new roommates. I remember looking into her face. My mother was dead and my dad was long out of the picture, so my siblings were my family. She looked at me knowing I was feeling awkward with her lingering with my new roommates. She knew I didn't really want her to go. But we knew it was time.

We don't forget these things.

Parents gradually lose control of their children as they age. It abruptly ends when they go to college. However, the commandment to "Honor your father and mother, that the days may be long upon the land which the Lord thy God gave you" gives a biblical basis for the relationship between parents and their children. In a general sense, this applies to all in authority over us (see Malachi 1:6, 1 Timothy 2:1-2, 1 Peter 2:17).

As children get older, we are left with prayer and wisdom. That sounds poetic, but praying for your child seems much less effective than scooping him or her out of a gathering of toddlers when misbehaving. Praying seems less effective than putting childproof locks on the cupboards and telling your children they have to go to bed. But prayer is an action and a means of grace that we retain after our hands can no longer intervene.

Prayer

Prayers range from the all night, heart-wrenching communion of Jesus in Gethsemane before he was to be crucified, to the brief prayer for guidance by the prophet Nehemiah before addressing his king. Because God knows our thoughts (Romans 8:26) we may wonder, "Why pray?" One answer is that we are commanded to pray. The other is to nurture ourselves with a communion with Christ. When we pray, we are approaching a holy God and can only do this by hiding behind Jesus, so that God sees the righteousness of Jesus and not our sinful state. This parallels the approach with that of the Old Testament priests who had to make many blood sacrifices and other physical preparations before approaching God.

We know from Jesus' guidance in the Lord's Prayer that we are to pray for God's "will to be done." That is the fundamental prayer. In John 14:14, Jesus says, "If you ask me anything in my name, I will do it." "My name" means we recognize the essence of who Jesus is and pray in that regard. While Jesus acts as our priest in speaking to the Father, it is the prayers that are in accordance with his will that are honored.

Consider the prophet Nehemiah's approach to handling a king's question. He was very anxious when he was addressed by the Persian king, Artaxerxes. Therefore, Nehemiah paused for the briefest time to pray to God. It was so brief, the king didn't seem to notice, as you can see in the following description of events described in Nehemiah 2:4-5: "The king said to me, "What is it you want?" Then I prayed to the God of heaven, and I said to the king…"

This is a delightful sequence of priorities. We learn that the king's servant, Nehemiah, addressed God before addressing his king. Nehemiah was probably doing what the Apostle Paul said in 1 Thessalonians 5:17, where we are guided to, "pray without ceasing."

We can rest our discussion of prayer by recognizing we are not like slaves, but rather sons and daughters of God (Galatians 4:7). Slaves feel like they have no right to do anything, but we can approach God and pray for good things for our children. We are not just lost in desperation rooted in fear. We can pray that our children will prosper, we can pray for abundance.

Because we are loved by God, we can pray big.

Crying to the Wind

I write poetry. It has been a refuge my whole life. Many people don't like to read poetry, they feel compelled to like it, even though it may be sappy or incomprehensible. But it is a voice for many of us. I will fearfully include a snippet of a simple poem put to song related to the empty nest that might be appealing. Below is one little verse and refrain from a song I wrote (with the chordal progression of D-A-Bm-G, the refrain is C-Bm-G):

Kiss my air and whisper sweet
Stories when I was the king
Kids would listen and I sing
We loved to do everything

Won't the memories play with dancing mind in every loving way. / Won't they sing to me and ring to me in gracious children's play.

Parden the indulgence, I have had to write so many poems....

Art, poetry, and journaling can be vehicles for crying out—along with coffee among friends and restful prayer.

Wisdom

Wisdom is such a broad idea that it can't be defined easily. The Bible says, "The fear of the Lord is the beginning of wisdom" (Proverbs 9:10). I saw this on a billboard a long time ago and I thought it was creepy. But it is true. The notion of wisdom could be replaced by love in this case. Or it could be called "informed action," which is a sweet term also.

Parents love their children. Wisdom is knowing how to apply that love. Parents love their children in a distinct way that lets them apply their wisdom most effectively. However, this can mean being silent or not taking action. Sometimes it's the opposite—parents speak directly to a problem or take some kind of interventional step. Who decides when it is most wise and loving to give a child advice or directly intervene in his or her life? It's the parent. No one else should presume to be more loving or more wise. Christian parents rely on the Bible to present truths that are most loving and most wise. And so, Christian parents pray, love, and read the Bible.

We are comforted also by God's promises, such as in Proverbs 22:6, "Train up a child in the way he should go; even when he is old he will not depart from it." We also recall the promise of Jeremiah 29:11: "For I know the plans I have for you, declares the Lord, plans for welfare and not for evil, to give you a future and a hope."

Parental Preparation

Our children's move to college still leaves us emotionally connected, but it can also leave us grievously separated. There is a balance between "giving them space" and "being there for them." It is presumptuous to think anyone except the parents have sufficient insight to make these calls. Your child probably knows many of these things and you don't need to lecture them as you see in their eyes that they want you to hurry up and finish your parental aphorisms.

Below are some ideas to consider. Some of these are done before going off to college, some of these are done every day they are gone.

- Tell your child you will pray for him or her every day.
- Pray for your children every day.
- Stay connected. You're an expert at this already. You know how to make phone calls, texts, and online video chats. You know how to write letters and cards. People keep handwritten things, they retain a special value. You know how to make and buy gifts. Making something is a gift of your time and, like a handwritten letter, holds a special meaning to the child. You know important dates in their life. Wisdom is needed as to whether you get

on social media or connect with your child on social media.

- Parents need to recognize behavioral lines that can't be crossed. When do they need to physically intervene or get someone to aid them? Sometimes the calvary needs to ride in. Sometimes it needs to stay parked in the driveway. Be wise!
- Educate your children about finances. Highlight important dates and the consequences of missing them, whether they be taxes, tuition payments or rent. Try to reduce these kinds of surprises. There are great resources out there for this. YouTube has replaced moms and dads in a lot of areas, and this might be one of them.
- Discuss personal security. Make sure they understand how to protect themselves from threats. They need to know how to avoid bad situations and how to remove themselves from toxic situations.
- Discuss identity theft, fraud, and computer security. There is a lot of information out there, and your child may well know more than you do. Maybe you can teach each other.
- Discuss the issues that will induce extra anxiety. This is a huge list and includes everything from peer pressure, Christian hypocrisy, and cheating to all the far ranging deplorable social activities in our culture. Internet filters are good. Don't let money be the guiding force in their life. Just because Amazon

Prime is appealing, it also presents objectionable movies for free. Saving money isn't always the goal. Encourage them to keep control of their personal environment (even if it cost them more) and model this behavior yourself.

- Share your stories. If you went to college, tell them some illuminating stories. You are not trying to scare them, so again wisdom is needed. Some stories are kept in reserve if they are ever needed.
- Life skills. If they haven't done their own laundry, they need to learn. If they have a car, they should know how to take care of it, including changing a tire. You know what needs to be done in this area.
- Coaching. Be on your child's side. Listen, let him or her vent. Encourage them in areas where you are confident in their abilities. If you are not confident in their abilities, give them advice on how to improve these abilities or how to follow a different, more fruitful path. Help them be wise.
- Family. Recognize the effect of a child's departure on siblings. Encourage him or her to speak honesty about how they feel and recognize the change in family dynamics when one child has left.

Below are some thoughts for your children who are entering the college culture.

Closing Recommendations for Students

- Recognize there will be a spiritual battle for your mind.
- Pray without ceasing.
- Read the Bible regularly.
- Join a local church.
- Maintain intimate, accountable connection with your "home" church.
- Prepare to be different. This is very difficult, but you will be respected.
- Understand epistemology and the logic of Christianity.
- Understand Christian apologetics. There are many good books on this topic. Many of these books are based on themes or use a question-and-answer style, which make them easy to use as a reference.
- Understand worldviews, bias, and hypocrisy. Christian hypocrisy is particularly hurtful. Although seen at a young age, it can flourish in a college environment.
- Join a campus ministry. Have friends that can talk about faith as easily as they talk about classwork.
- Be wary of residence halls and roommates. Generally, avoid residence halls and change roommates if there is a problem. The effect of student's living environment is powerful and insidious. However, a good roommate can be a

bulwark against the lowest common denominator prevailing. The best approach is to either 1) select your roommate carefully, 2) live off campus or 3) live in a single room. Living at a home might be an option for some.

- Be optimistic. College is an opportunity to grow intellectually and solidify your faith and understanding of the world. You have more energy and stamina than your professors, parents, and pastors—use it wisely.

11

For Professors

The students stare at me as I walk briskly into the classroom and over to the podium. I scan the room, not knowing where to rest my eyes. I purposefully arrived only a couple of minutes before the start of class to avoid the awkwardness of silence. I'm a little nervous. They're a little nervous. They clutch their phones for the comforting familiarity. So starts the first day of class.

My approach with new classes is to talk about frameworks for knowledge and this turns into the epistemological discussion of, "How do you know what you know?" This conversation provides a natural pivot to our personal position with respect to knowledge, information, and how we acquire truth.

My middle school insecurities seem to come out when I talk about my Christian faith. I want to be cool, hip, and relevant but I feel that speaking of my faith is anything but that.

Then I say something like, "I am a Christian and believe the Bible is true. It is the foundation upon which I stand and it is appropriate to be forthright with one's truth claims." I keep it short and snappy – students don't pay tuition to hear preaching. However, they recognize we all rest on some type of faith-based foundation.

Finally, at the end of that awkward first class, I put a box of books outside my room. I tell the students that my book[1] is free, but I warn them that it is an overtly Christian presentation. In my book I write about the wonderful outdoor adventures in our area, such as rock climbing, skiing, and sailing. Each of these topics has a Christian reflection. At the end of the little book, I have a short apologetics section.

It's a lot easier for me to set out a cardboard box full of small books than to have a heart-to-heart conversation with each student. Our Lord is gracious and can help reserved people like myself to present a personal testimony about our relationship with the living God.

Salvation comes from the Lord's love and mercy, not a professor's little book. However, we can present faith in an appropriate way that honors Christ and comforts fellow brothers and sisters among the students. However, we can be pushed back from our duty by fear of suffering and pride.

If God has put you in a position of authority over a young adult, you need to show Christ's love in your work and interaction. We remember in Matthew 18, when the disciples were arguing who was the greatest of them, Jesus told the disciples to humble themselves like a child. Jesus tells about the dire consequences for those who cause the vulnerable to sin. Later in Matthew 25, after he explains a string of parables, Jesus again uses the idea of the "least of these my brothers," saying that when we are in a position to help people, we must. Specifically, Jesus said: "Truly, I say to you, as you did it to one of the least of these my brothers, you did it to me" (Matthew 25:40). In Isaiah 5, God says, through the prophet Isaiah, that we need to watch for evil. We must not confuse good and evil. Specifically, Isaiah 5:20 says, "Woe to those who call evil good and good evil, who put darkness for light and light for darkness, who put bitter for sweet and sweet for bitter!"

The Bible tells us not to back down from the world. Moral relativism is a weak foundation for those who believe in a perfect truth. Some are blessed with faith and they can see this. The action plan regarding preaching biblical truths is presented clearly in 2 Timothy 4:2-5:

I charge you in the presence of God and of Christ Jesus, who is to judge the living and the dead, and by his appearing and his kingdom: preach the word; be ready in season and out of season; reprove, rebuke, and exhort, with complete patience and teaching. For the time is coming when people will not endure sound teaching, but having itching ears they will accumulate for themselves teachers to suit their own passions, and will turn away from listening to the truth and wander off into myths. As for you, always be sober-minded, endure suffering, do the work of an evangelist, fulfill your ministry.

"Accumulating for themselves teachers to suit their own passions." Isn't this our natural state, where we become our own god? Or at least surround ourselves with the echo chamber of our own desires. Dissonance will cause agitation.

Professors have to be prepared to suffer and defend their hope. Read how the Apostle Peter presents this:

Now who is there to harm you if you are zealous for what is good? But even if you should suffer for righteousness' sake, you will be blessed. Have no fear of them, nor be troubled, but in your hearts honor Christ the Lord as holy, always being prepared to make a defense to anyone who asks you for a reason for the hope that is in you; yet do it with gentleness and respect, having a good conscience, so that, when you are slandered, those who revile your good behavior in Christ may be put to shame. For it is better to suffer for doing good, if that should be God's will, than for doing evil. (1 Peter 3:13-17)

We are told to suffer when it is God's will. This is easy to read but extremely difficult to practice, especially when navigating tenure issues and the peculiar environment of academia.

I was a new, very assistant professor and campus ministry advisor, sitting in the biggest cafeteria on campus. I was with a bunch of campus ministry students and a pastor. The visiting pastor had brought in a long red ribbon, which we were unrolling across the center of the long table around which we were seated. The cafeteria was noisy, as hungry student filled up the cafeteria for lunch. The pastor was using a big voice. As I helped unroll the ribbon, I was feeling a cold sweat. I felt embarrassed as students throughout the cafeteria were watching and listening to us. I don't know what the pastor's message was about, but I remember feeling very awkward and vulnerable with my ribbon-adorned table and a big voice talking about Jesus. My pride, arrogance, and desire for status was burrowing deep into my stomach. And so, I write much about pride here. I think it is one of the main stumbling blocks with which professors contend.

The Problem of Pride

Even the most altruistic professor has to contend with the problem of pride. This was our original sin in the Garden of Eden. When George Orwell shared his reasons for writing, he had them in this order:

1. Sheer egoism. The desire to seem clever and to get talked about.
2. Aesthetic enthusiasm.
3. Historical impulse, desire for understanding.
4. Political purpose. To push the world in certain directions.

Augustine was more direct. He said, "Indeed, every other kind of sin has to do with the commission of evil deeds, whereas pride lurks even in good works in order to destroy them."

Pride is a problem discussed often in the Bible. King Uzziah of Judea became prideful in his success. 2 Chronicles 26:16 says, "But when he was strong, he grew proud, to his destruction." He ended up with leprosy and lived the isolated life of a leper.

David had to deal with his own pride and arrogance (see 2 Samuel 11). He spent the rest of his life apologizing for this (see the Psalms!). Before this problem, David had to deal with an authority figure (Saul) that was trying to kill him. Saul was the king of Israel and was jealous of David's success. So jealous, he wanted David killed. When David had the opportunity to kill Saul, he didn't (see 1 Samuel 24 and 26). He recognized Saul's authority and submitted to him. This is one of the marks of the Christian. Obeying authority is being a Christian witness. It is very, very difficult in a culture born of revolution and honors protesters and dissenters.

David waited patiently for his time. Working with authority figures who have different values, such as David cooperating with King Saul, is illustrative. We do what we can. Sometimes that means waiting. Waiting is tough. A helpful Bible narrative regarding patience is shown in Joseph's life story as told in Genesis 37-50. Joseph was loved by his father, but Joseph's brothers were jealous and sold him as a slave in Egypt. All sorts of bad things happen in Egypt, but Joseph ends up being the right-hand man of Pharoah and is put in a position to save his own family, including his father and the brothers that mistreated him. It is a great story to read for those suffering injustice and feel like they are on a downward spiral. Misery turns to good. Although you might not see the good in your lifetime, faithfulness glorifies God and is promised to be good for you.

Pride in the Classroom

Serving others is a kiss from the fingertips to the air. It is one of the most noble pursuits. But serving as a professor mixes intimately with pride. In *Glittering Vices*, philosopher Rebecca Konyndyk DeYoung confesses: "I lust after recognition, I am desperate to win all the little merit badges and trinkets of my profession, and I am of less real use in this world than any good cleaning lady."[2]

We don't want to confuse excellent teaching with just impressing students with our well-practiced vocabulary and harmonized concepts. I need a constant reminder about pride. It seems our profession encourages us to drift into becoming the unappealing know-it-all. We have to be on the alert for our own confirmation bias, where we favorably view opinions that agree with ours.

The following has been in my syllabus for a number of years and I try hard to follow it. The podium should not be used for unfair advantages. Faculty have opinions, but opinions on many topics can be unfairly imputed onto students.

Instructor Bias

My goal is that you learn how to think and not what to think. By its nature, design requires creative (and very human) approaches. These approaches can be influenced by tradition and an experientially rooted bias. Your educational experience should not include receiving any sort of instructor indoctrination.

Where controversial issues arise, I may present information from sources representing differing views from which you can develop your own opinion. These writings will be appropriate and professional presentations of the topics. However, unlike me, you have the right to present your opinions in class, which other students can debate. As an instructor with an unfair access to the podium, I do not share in that privilege. Think for yourself!

Besides pride being a problem of our fallen state, there are additional complications for professors. Many professors try to "produce" students who share their views. Professors may develop the goal of having their students think like them. This may seem reasonable if we profess expertise in a discipline. However, why should a student care about our opinion on anything? They can get opinions a lot cheaper elsewhere.

We can learn from great minds and those who have dedicated themselves tirelessly to their disciplines. However, throwing out quotes from "experts" is weak exposition. Where expert commentary is offered from the podium, it should be two opposing opinions thereby allowing students to struggle with what they believe. Our individual commentary is always connected with some intellectual ecology and worldview. When we contend with various viewpoints, our inclination is to side with the greater expert, which is lazy analysis.

We shouldn't aspire for students to quote us or remember our opinions. Students should only remember their own intellectual journey. Professors should be guides, like Dante's Virgil. Our vanity shouldn't be satiated by young minds, but rather we should be confident in the excellence of our teaching.

Nearly one hundred years ago, US President, Calvin Coolidge noted the problems with what he calls "self-worship." When people in authority are constantly assured of their greatness "they live in an artificial atmosphere of adulation and exaltation which sooner or later impairs their judgment. They are in great danger of becoming careless and arrogant."[3]

Comfort

We desire comfort, but what we need are sacrifice and trust. Comfort is appealing, but it placates people and destroys deeply human quests. It prevents difficult actions and difficult conversations as we hunker under comfort's false sense of security and bliss. Life is neither easy nor comfortable, but we love the low hanging fruit of comfort, where success is measured by minimal motion and minimal stress.

Comfort shouldn't be a way of life because it shifts its role from nurturing us to defeating us. Asceticism seems to live in all cultures and religions as people push back against comfort. However, hedonism thrives too, and many of us slither between asceticism and hedonism like a snake in a small alley.

Government

The government can provide no answers. The government is not the church. The biblical presentation of the government's role is that it can restrain evil. That's it. When Jesus said, "give onto Caesar that which is Caesar's," Jesus was also saying everything else is God's.

An example of the government doing good things for the church can be seen by extending the story we considered in Chapter 3, when the Apostle Paul was thrown out of the temple in Jerusalem for presenting something that the people didn't want to hear. However, there is more to that story. Not only was he thrown out of the temple, the people were going to kill him! This was stopped by the intervention of the governing tribune and his soldiers. They stopped the crowd from beating him (Acts 21:32). The tribune even allowed Paul to address the crowd (Acts 21:40).

I'm both a US and Norwegian citizen. Attending fourth-grade in Norway was unique. When the teacher came into our classroom, we stood up. The boys would bow and the girls would curtsey. We went to school six days per week. No one worked or even made noise on Sundays. When I was next in Norway, thirteen years later, everything changed. Marriage had weakened, Sunday was just another free day, and certainly no one bowed. Outward signs of deference to the Lord's Day or to authority fades with the whims of social trends. You recall the social history of much of the ancient world—they were very barbaric and lascivious. The "old days" weren't that great.

There was a time when the government was the church, for example the theocracy of Israel. However, that period cycled through good and bad rulers. Israel had tremendous problems with bad rulers doing bad things, including killing the prophets that God sent.

Secular universities usually have religious outreach programs. These are often a chaplaincy role that, at best, directs student to a clergy member. At worst, the office gives didactic teaching rooted in some collage of faiths. Students in emotionally vulnerable positions are not best served by this sort of chaplaincy. In contrast, some student organizations can do well in serving students. They often have much independence from the administration and have a more clear commitment to biblical truths. The challenge for chaplaincies is their divided interests. One is a commitment to their faith tradition, but the other is an obligation to their employer. This divided office is seen in prison and military chaplaincies also. Chaplains do not replace the church, or the overseers in the church.

In the end, organizations are not people, they do not have a moral code that stands up to any enduring scrutiny. They follow trends and laws. Some institutions get to create laws, but they do not carry any absolute truth behind them.

The book of Romans offers a Christian worldview into the role of government. Romans 13:1-5 says:

> Let everyone be subject to the governing authorities, for there is no authority except that which God has established. The authorities that exist have been established by God. Consequently, whoever rebels against the authority is rebelling against what God has instituted, and those who do so will bring judgment on themselves. For rulers hold no terror for those who do right, but for those who do wrong. Do you want to be free from fear of the one in authority? Then do what is right and you will be commended. For the one in authority is God's servant for your good. But if you do wrong, be afraid, for rulers do not bear the sword for no reason. They are

God's servants, agents of wrath to bring punishment on the wrongdoer. Therefore, it is necessary to submit to the authorities, not only because of possible punishment but also as a matter of conscience.

Discerning God's Will

I'm rather simple minded in regard to discerning God's will. I work with students, so I believe God wants me to work with students. God gave me all my abilities, including my intellectual ones, but I struggle constantly to understand God's will. It fights my lazy spirit that wants to sit and eat junk food.

Both our thoughts and actions have to be consistent with God's Word. We must also appreciate both the providential gifts and time we are working in. While God will equip us, we must recognize our special abilities that allow us to serve, while at the same time not cower under what we perceive as weaknesses that prevents us from serving. Are you sure you aren't gifted with dish washing and shovel digging? However, there are times in our lives when we are prevented from doing certain works. Paul and Silas are specifically "forbidden by the Holy Spirit to speak the word" in certain regions (Acts 16:6). At other times, Paul discerns God's will to serve in places that are not apparent openings, such as in Ephesus where so many adversaries awaited him as described in 1 Corinthians 16:7-9.

While Christian professors need to discern appropriate behaviors, they also need to do more than just their job. They need to glorify God. This is really tough in certain environments. We may tend to want to see physical signs of God's will, from the flame and smoke that led the Jews out of Egypt to Gideon looking for dew on the fleece he laid out.

Are there approaches to discerning God's will? We start with the Bible. We consider whether our actions are consistent with the Bible and whether we possess adequate abilities for what we are considering. We must also recognize the appropriate time for action. Lean on others too. Your brothers and sisters in Christ can help you with these inquiries. God will work in them also.

How Professors Can Help

- State your worldview, positionality, and epistemological approaches to the transcendent. You can share the fact that you are a Christian. This is intellectually honest because it impacts your worldview. You are not a teaching machine; you have beliefs and biases that should be honestly stated. I make it brief and I leave copies of my book, which I mentioned previously, outside the door so I don't see who takes it. This presentation of faith feels anti-intellectual and very awkward (for me, at least), which is why I have a whole chapter about suffering for Christ.

- Model Christ. This is a very bold and broad admonition, which comes from Scripture itself. As a professing Christian, you will be watched and tested. Be prepared.
- Create an uplifting environment. Stop profanity or other activities that are offensive.
- Don't create environments that encourage ethical challenges. Don't make tests with honor systems, these encourage cheating. Students are always several steps ahead of faculty and IT professionals. Students tell me that unproctored online exams only test your ability to use Google. Watch for confirmation bias, especially in grading. Make certain you recognize your propensity to want confirmation of your own ideas. Don't penalize students when they carry different ideas. Students are not paying for your opinions or beliefs, they are paying to enhance their own mind's abilities.

12

For Pastors

The church has the right to guide us in what we should believe, but the Holy Spirit piques our interest in learning about God and hearing his voice. So we don't just listen to the yelling of the crowd, the warmly-spoken words of social media influencers, or the actions of our heroes. The translation and interpretation of the Bible is the duty of the church, not the linguists at Yale, the philosophers at Oxford, or the archeologists at Columbia.

I'm not a pastor, but I write with great respect and affection for this challenging call. The burdens are immense and I propose to make them more so because I remind pastors that the Bible says God's pastors are obligated to shepherd their congregation. Peter is given the mandate three times to "feed my sheep" (John 21:17). More pointedly, Hebrews 13:17 says, "Obey your leaders and submit to them, for they are keeping watch over your souls, as those will have to a give an account."

Pastors can only speak biblical truths, but they must do this. If a young adult is a member of a parent's church, which is very common, the obligation doesn't end due to the distance and nomadic lifestyle of a college student. This may be especially frustrating when a pastor observes the empty-nested parents celebrating their "freedom" (my wife and I took a trip to New England.)

Pastors are asked to do a lot. Asking them to tend to young adults far from home seems an unfair burden. But that is the pastor's duty. Who else can call the student and ask about his or her spiritual life? Who can ask how they are handling the new culture? Perhaps it is church leadership with different titles than pastor, but the idea is the same. The young adult's home church is obligated to provide love and care until he or she transfers to another church.

R.C. Sproul asserts a high standard for pastors, writing:

[T]he pastor is called to tend the flock. Following again John's imagery from nature, when a sheep is wounded or becomes ill, it is to be noticed by the good shepherd, who takes that sheep from the flock and gives the special attention needed by the sheep to be restored to fullness of health. So it is that the good pastor is one who knows the aches, the pains, the joys, and the sorrows of each member of his congregation, so that he can tend to their needs and so that they aren't overcome by physical maladies or by spiritual and psychological distress. He is there to encourage the sheep and to see to it that they grow to the fullness of maturity in the life of Christ, conforming to Christ's very image.[1]

Mental health is a huge problem on campus. Saving faith is foundational for mental health. While many need additional services and medications, certainly God can heal distraught hearts. I have seen some people that want God to be a magic genie and solve their problems, so they dabble in Christianity. But Christians don't test God. They love him and accept his will in their lives.

Many different college ministries serve students. However, these parachurch organizations don't replace a home church. Churches need to recognize that college ministries don't have everything covered like you might assume. They deal with their own problems, including subtle power struggles and turf wars. Often they have to work across denominations and therefore remain silent about certain theological issues. As a long-time college ministry faculty advisor, I have been thrilled to observe the outpouring of love and generosity from our local churches. I have been contacted by many pastors simply asking how they can serve. Our community has richly offered food, fun, and laughter in Christian love.

What can pastors and churches do?

Below are some outreach ideas. If the student's "home" church is far away, it can't do all the things described below. But the church can do some of them. Fundamentally, you are trying to know the student's spiritual struggles and enter into this struggle with wisdom, love, and faith in God's promises.

- Pray for students by name.
- Treat them like adults. Ask them to serve the church.
- Write personal notes. Handwritten notes, demonstrate a sacrifice of time in a peculiarly attractive way. Gifts are always nice too!

Local churches can:

- Offer tutoring. Ask some of your gifted members to help with writing, math, and science topics. "Ask a

Mom" or "Ask a Dad" advisors can help fix things and solve problems; they can be a joyous refuge for a student. Students benefit from the mentoring of an older person.

- Make food and events. This has a long, beautiful tradition and can go in many creative directions.
- Offer social gatherings connected with student interests. Students gather for more than food events; their interests change with the years and range from gaming to outdoor adventures. See if you can be part of these.
- Share your resources. Churches can host study halls, club meetings, and makerspaces. They can even provide pickup trucks, vans, and tools.
- Rent out a room in your house. Carve a space out for a college student so your family can be a refuge.

13

Let's Make Things Better

What do we trust?

About a month ago, I went rock climbing in an area north of my home. I enjoy climbing and rappelling on these hidden cliffs I found many years ago. I have a routine. I park my car on a dirt road and hike up a steep mountain until I find my cliffs. I know to hike up a ways and turn left. I know after about ten minutes of hiking I won't hear the sound of the stream that cascades down a valley by the road where my car is parked. Later in the hike, I will hear a more powerful stream from another direction. These things are some of my guides when I search for these cliffs. I don't bring a compass or GPS with me.

This time I couldn't find my cliffs. I was humbled. I found some smaller cliffs and I climbed them. When I looked at the knots I used to set up the climb, I trusted them. Why do I trust them? Experts have said these are the right knots to use and they have worked for me in the past.

I was disappointed that I couldn't find my hidden cliffs. I headed back to my car. I couldn't see the sun through the trees. I couldn't hear any of my streams either, but I had an idea of which way to go. I hiked and hiked. I was expecting a steep descent that would drop me to the valley where I parked my car. I hiked in what I thought was a straight line, but I wasn't descending at all.

I realized I was lost.

Humbled again. Then I felt stupid that I was so arrogant that I didn't bring a compass with me. Because the trees are so similar and I couldn't see landmarks from under the canopy of trees, it was hard to be sure I was hiking a straight line. I literally said out loud, "Jesus, you've got this one." One of the funny things about this experience was I felt more embarrassed than afraid. How vain can I be?

Eventually, I intersected a dirt road that I recognized. I walked to a beautiful cliff I knew was nearby this road and rappelled down. I packed up my gear under a cloudy, darkening sky and hiked along the dirt road that promised to deliver me to my car. I arrived at my car as darkness swelled the valley.

Why do I share this? Pride is so powerful it can displace truth and reason. I trust my rope and climbing equipment because of quality assurance implied by the right stamps and stickers on the gear. I trust the knots I tie because I have trusted them in the past. I trusted my sense of direction and ability to recognize the land around me. Obviously, that failed this time. My equipment did not fail me, but my mind did.

Why do I have trust like this? I don't even trust my climbing abilities, otherwise I wouldn't be using ropes to catch me if I fall. In other words, there is a difference between being confident you can do something, or at least optimistic that you can overcome obstacles, and trusting that something is true.

Proverbs 3:5-6 says, "Trust in the Lord with all your heart and lean not on your own understanding; in all your ways submit to him, and he will make your paths straight." You have to trust in something. If you are blessed with faith, you trust in God's message to us in the Bible. All our obstacles are approached under the imposition of prayer and biblical truths.

The Heart

In 1980, the prolific author and chemist, Isaac Asimov wrote:

There is a cult of ignorance in the United States, and there has always been. The strain of anti-intellectualism has been a constant thread winding its way through our political and cultural life, nurtured by the false notion that democracy means that 'my ignorance is just as good as your knowledge.'[1]

We often form opinions without knowing the governing principles for our actions. Should George Washington have pushed for freeing the slaves as he took on the role of our first President? Was the James Webb telescope worth the money? Who forms the governing principles? Is this the role of college?

As students recast themselves as adults, they look for people to emulate and ideals to pursue. They can find these at college. Do we want colleges to replace churches for moral guidance?

Truth gives us a lamp. This truth is not for private introspection but for public declaration. Obedience, not knowledge, is the vehicle of Christian transformation. Jesus said, "If you abide in my Word, you are truly my disciples" (John 8:31). What does *abide* mean? It means "act in accordance with," as in never separating, so that we speak, act, and think in accordance with the Bible. Tough to do? Yes, indeed. And so we need to repent when we fail, but we don't give up striving. We shouldn't celebrate our biblical knowledge and forfeit our biblical-directed action.

Proverbs 4:23 says, "Keep your heart with all vigilance, for from it flow the springs of life." The New International Version translation says, "Above all else, guard your heart, for everything you do flows from it." Perhaps that is more clear.

Young people have their hearts and minds under assault by many forces. They must guard their hearts and we must help. We must trust what we believe, we must use the positions of authority in which we have been entrusted to prepare the student for the road ahead.

Philosophers Jean-Jacques Rousseau and Friedrich Nietzsche argued for the natural goodness of people. This sounds appealing, but are people naturally good? Rousseau thought that society perverts us by compelling us to conform to its ways. He thought the individual was great, and society was flawed and hurtful. Therefore, the individual's feelings have the greatest value, and our personal definition of good and evil are the basis for truth claims. This thinking leads promptly to Nietzsche's *Ubermensche*, a superman who lives by his own standards.

These philosophical notions are contrary to biblical teaching. In Jeremiah 17: 9-10, we are told, "The heart is deceitful above all things, and desperately sick; who can understand it?" When grieving at Gethsemane,

Jesus did not succumb to his feelings of fear, but persevered to do his Father's will and die on a cross. The inaction of Jesus as he grappled with his emotions is difficult to understand. We want to take action and be masters of our destiny. Maybe this is why we have more people fighting for God (like the Apostle Peter in Luke 22) than dying for God (like Stephen in Acts 7)—the mob of zealous crusaders stumbling over the bodies of silent martyrs. Silent suffering seems to chomp on the human spirit.

Being silent in the noise can sometimes be wise. The prophet Obadiah hid one hundred prophets in caves to protect them from the evil King Ahab's wife, Jezebel. (1 Kings 18:4). Obadiah gave them bread and water as they huddled and waited. Imagine hiding in a cave not knowing if you would ever be able to serve as you were called. All the while, you are in fear for your life and subsisting on bread and water! Do you think your waiting is more difficult?

We often feel powerless. We feel we are being hidden in a cave for some great purpose to which God has called us. However, we have no assurance of what we will be called to do. Maybe it is encouraging others. Maybe it has already passed. Maybe it was the conversation you had with a friend when you were twelve. Maybe your service is done, and now you hide in a cave, praying. But maybe not—Abraham and

Moses were old men when God called them to serve. It's not your choice.

We come out of hiding at some point. After Obadiah hid God's prophets, the prophet Elijah confronted King Ahab and the prophets of Baal. When Elijah meets Ahab, he doesn't hold back. Elijah says to the king, "[Y]ou have abandoned the commandments of the Lord and followed the Baals" (1 Kings 18:18). We see this "waiting in caves" when we earlier considered Esther's life. She waited for her time to serve. When she was needed, she did the right thing (see Esther 4:14).

When and how to serve God is a matter of discernment. However, if we only serve our own ambition and our own goals, we are like psychopaths. Adolf Hitler would agree with the adage, "If it feels good, do it." When our goals are rooted in the ephemeral values of a college culture, we end up ruling over a diaphanous wash of nothingness. The goals will drift. They will be far different in the future and you will always be one step behind. A long-time friend of mine identifies himself as being the most liberal person in any gathering. His standards keep moving as he struggles to keep up. When Ronald Reagan was shot, my friend's comment was the assassin "should have used a bigger gun." His self-directed identity was preserved.

Our goals fit into a box bracketed between ambition and pride. Being ambitious is good in many ways.[2] For Christians, the connection between ambition and pride is a challenging dilemma with which we struggle. Pride leads to self-reliance and therefore to self-destruction. Pride motivated Adam and Eve to sin. Jesus recognized those who are spiritually weak and have a humble notion of themselves, saying, "Blessed are the poor in spirit, for theirs is the kingdom of heaven" (Matthew 5:3). The poor in spirit need to rely on Jesus fully. Recognizing that our accomplishments, abilities, and goals are God-given produces thankfulness, which is the first step in handling the dilemma of ambition versus pride. We ask ourselves, "Where do our ambitions point?" Often there is not a clear-cut answer.

In addition to struggling with the definition of what is ambitious and what is prideful, we have other semantic issues with the meaning of *heart* and *feelings*. I had an unusual occurrence many years ago. I intersected into the life of two people who were found to be pedophiles. By God's providence they turned up in my life as friends, one of whom was in a Christian group. Both of them were legally convicted and punished for their actions. However, as their friend, I knew they felt, and continued to feel, they were not doing anything wrong. They felt it was the way they were. So said their heart.

Just because one feels one is made a certain way or proclaims a personal morality doesn't make it true.

So who decides what is morally acceptable? Elected governments? Unelected judges? Unelected college administrations? Culture? For Christians, morality is a matter of a renewed heart and obedience. The Bible presents God's will, and the church is authorized to act as the vehicle for biblical application.

How do we harmonize protecting our heart "for from it flow the springs of life" and protecting against it because it is "deceitful above all things, and desperately sick"? You do it by comparing your heart against the Bible. Romans 12:1-2 says that your body is a "living sacrifice" and that we must "not be conformed to this world, but be transformed by the renewal of your mind." We don't judge by comparing to others, because they are all struggling too. While it can be good to have heroes, all heroes are tragic failures, except for Jesus. You may find people who act heroically or are models of Christian virtue in some way. But the leash is short and the hypocrisy is close to the surface. Only Jesus can be a model of sanctified human behavior. And it is by reading the Bible that we can renew our minds.

In the struggle to discern God's will, we strive to make useful contributions and allow this powerful beast of humanity to add to the wonder of the world. But our contributions should be for tomorrow. We need to sacrifice our narrow pretentions in favor of something eternal and good. We embrace the awkwardness of our position in current culture as we ground ourselves in God's everlasting promises.

This writing has been more passionate and personal than my normal work. Consequently, I have been harsher on my profession and the college environment than what might be appropriate. However, my writing is rooted in affection for students and their education. However, I am tempered by the admonition in 2 Timothy to be winsome in presenting my faith and living my life:

> So flee youthful passions and pursue righteousness, faith, love, and peace, along with those who call on the Lord from a pure heart. Have nothing to do with foolish, ignorant controversies; you know that they breed quarrels. And the Lord's servant must not be quarrelsome but kind to everyone, able to teach, patiently enduring evil, correcting his opponents with gentleness. God may perhaps grant them repentance leading to a knowledge of the truth, and they may come to their senses and escape from the snare of the devil, after being captured by him to do his will (2 Timothy 2:22-26).

Sometimes ideas need to be pondered before taking root. That takes time. A debate demands an immediate reply, but truth grounded in faith accepts the need for time in reflection and inner musing.

The Future

Colleges need to more fully respond to their status change from exclusive institutions for the privileged to sources of mass education. There is a demand for deep, textured learning that works the mind to its richest potential in terms of critical thinking and penetrating insights. However, there is a demand for education that moves people into satisfying careers. The educational approaches to these should be different. The first track, critical thinking, benefits from an immersive environment. The ideal is that the discussions in the classroom are followed by reading difficult, challenging texts then continuing the debate with roommates in the residence hall. The second track, vocational training, is some mixture of online learning, virtual labs, face-to-face lectures, physical labs, and practical internships.

Education is often pursued through YouTube videos and the other online resources at our fingertips. Moreover, AI systems will generate papers for students with a brief typed or spoken request. Ask an AI program to: "Write a two-thousand-word paper about medicine in China. Use college level writing," and see what happens. This is the way the world is—laced with short, easily accessible snippets of graphically presented information. Whether this is the best way to learn things or not is beyond my understanding. My opinion is that something is lost in the blurred cacophony. The diaphanous wash of recalled memories, interlinked ideas, and personal discovery seem to be lost under the assault of the internet's brief, curated, declarative statements. We are shouted at and presented color graphics. This seems unfortunate for those of us who plowed through thick books with dense narration and non-color-coded mathematics. But we take the world as it is and not how we want it to be. Young people will do fine and prosper in ways we can't imagine as they cast off the old shackles that slowed them down and create futures founded in their dreams.

I previously quoted Charles Malik, former President of the United Nations General Assembly, regarding the importance of the university. But the university has to adapt. The grand tradition of the academy will starve if it loses its way and becomes an indoctrinational vessel rather than a system of education that focuses on the mind's wonderful abilities and allows thinking to flourish. This slow starvation reminds me of the African fable about the mouse and the elephant.

The elephant had destroyed the mouse's nest several times so the mouse studied the elephant and learned how dependent he was on his trunk. When the elephant fell asleep, the mouse crawled into the elephant's trunk. The elephant could not dislodge the mouse from his trunk and the elephant finally succumbed to thirst and hunger.

Higher education has deep roots and has provided wonderful opportunities. Colleges provide a platform for ambitious students to learn the interconnected tapestry of their world and the foundations for their profession. However, college education is moving closer to satisfying vocational needs and further from allowing truth claims that accept faith as a valid component. College's often nurture worldviews contrary to, and contemptuous of, Christianity. This attitude is encouraged by Christian churches that waver on the status of the Bible.

Just like Petrarch, we seek moral truth among the corruption around us. If one institution doesn't provide moral truths, we will seek another. Educational alternatives will develop with time. For example, the educational experience of Christian students could be improved by some of the following ideas:

- Community pods. Create physical communities that avail themselves of all the online college programs available. Students would be physically present in some space, such as a Christian camp. Students will have a richer college experience by being physically present with fellow students then being alone on a computer. This environment encourages inquiry, conversation, and debate in ways that can't be orchestrated. Social learning is powerful.

- External, independent evaluation of coursework to check for bias. Professors should have no fear of other parties inspecting their coursework. This would not infringe on academic freedom, an independent party would only evaluate, not critique or recommend anything. External critiques already exist informally on the internet, but anonymous yelling is not very fair to faculty.

- Empower high school teachers. High school teachers do a great job of teaching—my high school teachers were far better teachers than my college professors (or me, for that matter). High schools provide a liberal arts education that exposes students to far ranging topics and ideas. How much history does an accountant need? Was their high school history that bad that they have to take more history courses in college? High school coursework that is unrelated to a student's major should be readily accepted if it meets college requirements.

Closing Comments

Sacrificial love is the mark of a Christian because it models what Jesus taught us and demonstrated with his own life. We don't like to carry this burden, but we persevere under it. We carry our burdens imperfectly as our feet plod through muddy paths. But we move forward. We try.

When our children were young, we couldn't imagine releasing them into the crazy world around us. We loved it when we were the center of their lives. We could make them smile by making a funny noise. We could brighten their faces with a promise of a day full of fun and play. Sacrificial love is most easily rendered by parents. It's buried in our nature and fueled by our powerful love. Parents protected their children, guided them, and taught them. Then they leave? They leave for a college campus? So we sink to our knees and pray, clawing at God's mercy and clinging to God's promises.

Professors get to stand in front of a class. We look out at faces that are many decades younger than our own. We are there because we promise an education. We are part of a system students go through to sharpen their minds and earn college degrees. As part of the system of higher education, we get to create a learning environment and assess how well they learn what we are teaching. But we are children of God and the way we think is rooted in our faith. Should we not be honest about that? Should our lives not be consistent with our hearts? Who put us in a position to teach students? Who gave us the abilities to do the job? Who gave us intelligence? So we do not preach, but we speak of our ontological and epistemological frameworks, and live a life worthy of our calling.

Pastors have wide ranging responsibilities that tax their time and their commitments. When a student goes off to college, he or she is especially vulnerable. Pastors have to watch that being out of sight is not being out of mind. The relationship between a pastor and a young person is very important and no other person will ever be respected in the same way. Pastors live in a student's mind. They represent a standard of living. They represent a servant of God.

Parents will love their children, Christ will preserve his church, and Christian faith is enduring. Therefore, ambitious, young people will find their way in the world without losing their footing. The simple message offered here is that parents must pray for their children, professors must be a light for Christ to their students, and pastors must shepherd their flock. And a butterfly lifts from an open hand and flutters up into the cool wind.

NOTES

Chapter 2

1. "Employment Projections: Education and Training Data." *Bureau of Labor Statistics*, 2021,
www.bls.gov/emp/documentation/education-training-system.htm.
2. "Employment Projections: Education Pays." *Bureau of Labor Statistics*, 2021, www.bls.gov/emp/chart-unemployment-earnings-education.htm.
3. "Pew Research Center's Social & Demographic Trends Project."
Pew Research Center, 2016, www.pewresearch.org/social-trends/2016/10/06/3-how-americans-view-their-jobs/#fnref-22108-24.
4. Dostoevsky, *The Brothers Karamazov*, New York: Macmillan, 2002.

Chapter 3

1. Mousavizadeh, Philip. *"A 'proliferation of administrators': faculty reflect on two decades of rapid expansion."* Yale News, June 21, 2022,
www.yaledailynews.com/blog/2021/11/10/reluctance-on-the-part-of-its-leadership-to-lead-yales-administration-increases-by-nearly-50-percent/.
Additional information, while dated, on this ratio is available at:
www.wwu.edu/accreditation/2014/documents/2.A.11(a)_Faculty_Administrators_Ratio.pdf.

Chapter 4

1. Jones, Jeffery. "U.S. Church Membership Falls Below Majority for First Time." March 29, 2021, Gallup News, https://news.gallup.com/poll/341963/church-membership-falls-below-majority-first-time.asp.

Chapter 6

1. *"Charles Malik", https://en.wikipedia.org/wiki/Charles_Malik*

2. "University Records and Life in the Middle Ages" tr. L. Thorndike, N.Y. 1975, 36, https://hdl.handle.net/2027/heb.06048

3. Hutchins, Robert Maynard. "Education for Freedom," Louisiana State University, 1943, 100, https://archive.org/details/in.ernet.dli.2015.501404/page/n109/mode/2up.

4. "US to fine for-profit colleges for false promises about graduates' prospects." Reuters, October 6, 2021, https://www.reuters.com/world/us/us-fine-for-profit-colleges-false-promises-about-graduates-prospects-2021-10-06/.

5. *South Dakota v. Dole*, 483 U.S. 203 (1987).

6. Schein, Edgar H. *Organizational Culture and Leadership*. San Francisco: Jossey-Bass, 1988, 81.

7. "Worst Colleges for Free Speech: 2022," Foundation for Individual Rights and Expression (FIRE), February 2, 2022, https://www.thefire.org/10-worst-colleges-for-free-speech-2022/. Some other organizations, such as the Southern Poverty Law Center, offer a different view on acceptable limitations of speech. They make their case with care and good intensions. An example can be seen at: https://www.splcenter.org/news/2017/10/26/splc-senate-colleges-must-uphold-free-speech-can-denounce-racist-speakers.

8. "Speech on Campus," American Civil Liberties Union (ACLU), https://www.aclu.org/other/speech-campus.

9. Cedeno Laurent, Jose G et al. "Influence of the residential environment on undergraduate students' health." *Journal of exposure science & environmental epidemiology* vol. 30,2, 2020, 320-327. doi:10.1038/s41370-019-0196-4.

10. Weaver, Rheyanne. "Understanding Peer Pressure in College: Why Fitting in Can Sometimes Hurt." Her: Women's Health and Fitness, July 22, 2010, https://www.empowher.com/mental-health/content/understanding-peer-pressure-college-why-fitting-can-sometimes-hurt.

11. "APA Dictionary of Psychology." American Psychological Association, 2022, https://dictionary.apa.org/normative-influence.

12. DeCremer, David. "Effect of Group Identification on the Use of Attributions." *The Journal of Social Psychology* 140, 2000, 267-69.

13. DeCremer, David, Mark van Vugt, and Jonathan Sharp. "Effect of Collective Self-Esteem on Ingroup Evaluations." *The Journal of Social Psychology* 139, 1999, 530-32.

Chapter 7

1. Curtis, Ken, "The Spread of the Early Church," May 3, 2010, https://www.christianity.com/church/church-history/timeline/1-300/the-spread-of-the-early-church-11629561.html.

2. Tozer, A. W. *Evenings with Tozer*, Chicago: Moody Publishers, Gerald B. Smith (Ed.), 1981. June 7.

Chapter 8

1. Bacon, Francis, "The Four Idols" In *The World of Ideas, 6th Edition*, Lee Jacobus (Ed.) Boston: Bedford/St. Martin's, 2002), 420.

2. See also discussions of positivism and constructivism. The parsing of these categories goes on endlessly, but these concepts are largely an evaluation of how we actually obtain knowledge as well as the validity and application of that knowledge.

3. Hilgevoord, Jan and Uffink, Jos. "The Uncertainty Principle." In *The Stanford Encyclopedia of Philosophy*, Spring 2014 Edition, Edward N. Zalta (Ed.), 2014. https://plato.stanford.edu/archives/spr2014/entries/qt-uncertainty.

4. Feyerabend, P. "Against method." New York: Verso, 1993.

5. Groh, S. *Beyond the brain: Birth, death, and transcendence in psychotherapy.* Albany, NY: State University of New York, 1985.

6. For example, Richard Rorty. Rorty, R. *The American Intellectual Tradition*, 3rd Ed, Ed. Hollinger, David A and Capper, Charles, Oxford University Press, 1997, 393.

Chapter 11
1. The book I am referencing is entitled, *Natural Grace: God and nature in our slice of Pennsylvania.*
2. DeYoung, Rebecca Konyndyk. *Glittering Vices*, 2ed, Grand Rapids, Michigan: Brazos Press, 2020.
3. Calvin Coolidge Presidential Foundation, "Quotations," https://coolidgefoundation.org/quote/quotations-w/.

Chapter 12
1. Sproul, RC. "What Does It Mean to Be a Shepherd Over the Flock?" October 4, 2017, https://www.ligonier.org/learn/articles/what-does-it-mean-be-shepherd-over-flock.

Chapter 13
1. Asimov, Isaac, "A Cult of Ignorance," *Newsweek, My Turn*, January 21, 1980, https://aphelis.net/wp-content/uploads/2012/04/ASIMOV_1980_Cult_of_Ignorance.pdf.
2. Many argue that ambition is not good, for example, the British statesman and philosopher, Edmund Burke, and American poet and essayist, Ralph Waldo Emerson. Emerson said it was one of the "great enemies of peace." Shakespeare's Macbeth expresses a common theme in literature where the hero falls due to pride and "excessive" ambition.

Made in the USA
Columbia, SC
08 October 2024

5de406ef-7bb8-4608-90b8-5f3bb0393eecR01